Ebony Wadlington

"I AM"
My Affirmations

Ebony Wadlington

Pearly Gates Publishing, LLC, Harlem, Georgia (USA)

"I AM" My Affirmations

"I AM" My Affirmations

Copyright © 2022
Ebony Wadlington

All Rights Reserved.
In accordance with the U.S. Copyright Act of 1976, the scanning, uploading, and electronic sharing of any part of this book without the author's or publisher's permission is unlawful piracy and theft of the author's intellectual property. If you would like to use material from this book (other than brief quotations for literary reviews), we ask you to please cite your reference.
Thank you for your support of the author's rights.

Photo credit: Delandren "DeFoto" Davis

Print ISBN 13: 978-1-948853-55-2
Digital ISBN 13: 978-1-948853-56-9
Library of Congress Control Number: 2022915917

Pearly Gates Publishing, LLC
Angela Edwards, CEO
P.O. Box 639
Harlem, GA 30814
BestSeller@PearlyGatesPublishing.com

What Others Are Saying...

"People say blood is thicker than water. That is true, but not for everyone. As far back as I can remember, as a young girl, I was always excited when my uncle and his family returned home from Texas. While I was excited to see them, I was filled with immense joy to see Ebony. She and I always had a special connection. I look back at old photos and see that I was always smiling and looking at her. She has always been someone who I looked up to. I have always known Ebony to be a fun, dancing, loving, and strong person. Even though I have known her all my life, I truly got to know her over the last few years. Her growth over the last couple of months has been remarkable. She may not have seen it her whole life, but I have always marveled at the strong spirit in her. The last conversation we had just a month ago, I couldn't envision it happening a few years ago. Ebony now knows her worth and who she is.

"When Ebony asked me if she should start an affirmation book, I told her that would be a good idea. The first day she sent me an affirmation, it made me look even further into myself and those things I had already been doing. I know if her words of affirmation can reach me, many others will be reached and blessed just the same. When she and I started exchanging affirmations, self-evaluations took place. I genuinely feel if these words can touch me the way they did her and me, they can touch thousands through this book.

I'm oh so proud of who Ebony has become and is becoming. Her future is bright. The sky is the limit for her. Whatever she puts her mind to, I know she can do it with God by her side."

~ **Jessica Wadlington**

"With every moment, you are making choices. Surrounding yourself with like-minded, spiritually-connected human beings creates a whirlwind of power. You must be accountable for your thoughts, have your ego take a back seat, and let your soul shine through. You and I are one when you shine. The same is true in the reverse. When we uplift one another, our lights attract more illuminating souls. Ebony's voice is one that some may not hear but needs to be read by others. Every affirmation is a lesson to work toward and acknowledge. Self-healing is essential, and I believe that thought alone is a beautiful blessing. Ebony has created a magnetic hold on me from the moment she passed through my life, and it's been 20 years. We remain connected no matter the ups and downs, ebbs and flows. On those days when I feel lost, I know I can vent to her or reconnect. I can read an affirmation and quickly get right back on my path. Ebony is someone I want by my side, creating more pathways for others to join."

~ **Tamera Carter**

"My connection with Ebony began to strengthen in 2017. At the time, we were building and seeing what our interests were. Very quickly, I realized she was experiencing a spiritual walk. What I know absolutely about Ebony is her passion for doing great things. In 2017, I almost lost my life. Ebony kept me motivated, encouraged, and optimistic. That mindset for her evolved into providing positive affirmations unknowingly. When she noticed her words were impactful and life-changing, she began sharing with close family and friends with a purpose. That was when her affirmations were conceived. Likening the process to a pregnancy, Ebony's affirmations were the birthing that led to countless others that flowed like the rivers and the seas. God is indeed using her through her obedience, as many of her affirmations have touched me personally. While the journey continues for Ebony, the walk is just the beginning. There are more affirmations to come!

~ **Lettia Morgan**

"Ebony and I met at Texas Southern University in the Respiratory Therapy program. She and I already had our own circle of friends, so we weren't looking to make new ones—but it's definitely what we found! We have always had a way of uplifting and supporting one another, whether in school or in life. Ebony and I would always seek out each other for clarification or understanding about one thing or another. We always give the most positive and honest parts of ourselves in our friendship. It's funny when I look back now, but affirmations have always been something we shared. We always knew when the other needed a few words of encouragement. Ebony being an only child has taught her to lean into those who carry only the most positive energy. The blossoming and growth I have seen within her are so apparent. She is a light. She is the seed. She is growth in the flesh."

~ **Kelli Evans**

"From the moment I met Ebony, I could tell she had a beautiful, sincere, and laid-back spirit. That belief hasn't changed. The more I got to know her, I noticed she was in her head a lot or just in her own zone. She could have been thinking about something troubling her while seemingly enjoying herself, or she could have been enjoying the vibe and observing/taking in the atmosphere. I know Ebony has been dealt some lessons in life and love (not from a place of naivety, but from being genuine) that some of us must learn the hard way. Her trials have made her stronger and wiser, just as they should. To see her flourishing now is an amazing sight to behold. Ebony is a lovely woman who honestly deserves all the good she does to be reciprocated, no matter how it manifests. Her affirmations reignited a positivity in me that I hadn't had since my sister passed. Ebony may not have known the impact her weekly words had, but I attest they were truly monumental for me."

~ **Trey Johnson**

"I AM" My Affirmations

Dedications

I dedicate this book to my grandfather,
IRA B. WADLINGTON,
who told me,
"KEEP YOUR HEAD IN THEM BOOKS!"

I also dedicate this book to all the amazing men and women I have met and those I have yet to meet who battle in the dark. Remember this:
*** The light shines!***

Ebony Wadlington

Acknowledgments

I first would like to express my deepest gratitude to my Heavenly Father—my Warrior Agent—for His never-ending love, guidance, and protection.

Completing this book was not the simplest task, but it was more rewarding than I thought. None of this would be possible without:

My parents who demonstrated their never-ending love and devotion. They stood by me during every struggle and all my successes.

I am eternally grateful for my family from Detroit, Michigan, and Oxford, Mississippi.

For inspiring me: Jessica Wadlington, Lettia Morgan, Martin Brown, Falecia Ann Foreman M.S., Tamera Carter, Belan Hamilton, Ciara Kaiser, Sylvia Brown, Quentin Williams, Kesha Stennis, Syndii Jenkins, Tanya Stanton, Danielle Brown, and my professor, Dr. Selina Ahmed.

For being a constant support: Tamara Byrd, Cherita Fuller, Melissa Chatman, Darius Sanders, Jessica Thomas, Tamara Coleman, Michael Lance Oliver Sr., Joie Brown, Jade Horton, Trey Johnson, Calon Mask-Oats, Monique "Mz. Moe" Young, and Steven Sullivan.

For giving me a place to rest my head when I did not have my own: Ashley Taylor, Kelli Evans, and Alicia Roland. I remember sleeping in my mom's living room while in school pursuing my second degree and napping in my car during breaks.

Demetrius Nash, who taught me about living an intentional life and for respecting and sustaining me in ways that I never knew I needed.

Windsor Village United Methodist Church Praise Dance Ministry for adopting me as their little and big sister.

And finally, to those who are still a part of my journey, even during the COVID-19 pandemic: Linda Horton, Ingrid Hargrove, Charra Cravens, Teonna (my Loc-titian), Patrice Starnes, Jeremy Dotson, and my co-workers.

Thanks to everyone on my publishing team who helped make this book a reality and get it into the hands of the readers.

Ebony Wadlington

Foreword

I was just getting home from a long day at work. As I pulled into my driveway, a long-time family friend was walking by. Kelli mentioned that her friend was interested in working for WIC (Women, Infants, and Children) for Harris County, so she asked if I was hiring.

"Tell your friend to apply," I replied.

During the interview process, I met a young lady who desired to learn, grow, and help others. While interviewing her, I learned she was my long-time family's friend's friend. (I knew I was going to hire her before finding that out.)

I always remember my talks with Ebony. She's very receptive and vulnerable towards things that are true, like the Word of God. When no one is looking, Ebony is. She observes and senses like no other. She takes in what she admires. Let me explain what I mean.

Ebony orchestrated and organized meetings to encourage her co-workers. She would leave nutritious snacks, such as strawberries, in the breakroom, along with a positive note. While working, we could hear her humming or singing in the hallways.

That was and is Ebony. She is a light on her feet, and by this and all that I previously said, she adapted and collaborated well with others.

While working with Ebony, I discovered she is eager to learn, despite the challenges. She is beaming. How? Not only does she beam light physically, but her mental and emotional intelligence shine brighter. She is optimistic because she always tries to see the good in things and people. She is a natural. For example, when given an assignment, she goes with the flow and tackles it like it is a piece of cake. Last but not least, she yearns for truth—which is to BE and LIVE as her authentic self, always.

~ **Felicia Ann Foreman, M.S.**

Preface

God had given me an assignment that started with breadcrumbs. It's unbelievable to me that His plans are always way bigger than our own. Realizing mental health issues are real on all levels, I had to be willing to let go of anything and anyone. I had reached a point in my life where it felt like the walls were closing in. In July 2022, I started sending text messages to inspire, encourage, and uplift not only me but also those connected to me—and I did so consistently.

Sidebar: You never know who is silently going through a battle. They could benefit from a random message or just knowing you were on their mind. You give what you would like to receive. Name one thing God has NOT pulled you through. I encourage you to celebrate even the smallest of wins. Doing what you have never done can be rewarding. Who knew the person to save you was YOU?

Things that once bothered me no longer fill that space. It's about what we feed our minds, bodies, and souls. We all have gifts. Take care of them. Trust that someone is advocating for you. Do not take anything personally. What others do has nothing to do with you. Once you become immune to the negativity of others, you will longer fall victim to needless suffering. If you can't get over it, going through it is a necessity.

This is my journey. I'm sharing it with you. Find your voice. Share your story. **YOU MATTER!**

Introduction

God has been so good to me. When I think I can do it all by myself or find a way to fix it alone, that is not the case. God has sent some amazing people into my life. Together, they have taken my broken pieces, glued my hope back together, and stood beside me as if there were no more cracks. In some way, I am inspired by every person I have met—especially those who radiate with love and have a zest for life!

I pray the following affirmations remind you of your power and grace. Remind yourself that your heart is filled with peace and love. Encourage yourself in knowing that each day will be as refreshing as the next.

Lastly, affirm daily: **"I AM..."**

Table of Contents

What Others Are Saying... vi

Dedications ix

Acknowledgments x

Foreword xii

Preface xiv

Introduction xv

Day One 1

Day Two 2

Day Three 3

Day Four 4

Day Five 5

Day Six 6

Day Seven 7

Day Eight 8

Day Nine 9

Day Ten 10

Day Eleven 11

Day Twelve 12

Day Thirteen 13

Day Fourteen 14

"I AM" My Affirmations

Day Fifteen 15

Day Sixteen 16

Day Seventeen 17

Day Eighteen 18

Day Nineteen 19

Day Twenty 20

Day Twenty-One 21

Day Twenty-Two 22

Day Twenty-Three 23

Day Twenty-Four 24

Day Twenty-Five 25

Day Twenty-Six 26

Day Twenty-Seven 27

Day Twenty-Eight 28

Day Twenty-Nine 29

Day Thirty 30

My "I AM" Affirmations 31

About the Author 37

Ebony Wadlington

"I AM" My Affirmations

Day One

Pack your bags! We are going on an adventure—on a path where it's all about your "Inner G"!

Self-Love

Self-Healing

Self-Forgiveness

Self-Care

Self-Confidence

Self-_____(fill in the blank)

To access your ticket, all you must do is...
LOVE ON YOU!

You are ENOUGH!

You are WORTHY!

You are AUTHENTIC!

You are FLAWLESS!

You are THE ONE!

∫ *One morning, I looked in the mirror and realized I was a human being who needed to be worked on from the inside out. I realized the journey would not be easy but well worth it.* ∫

Ebony Wadlington

Day Two

I release procrastination, doubt, negative energy, worry, stress, and pain.

I release any rising negativity against me and return it to the sender.

I release insecurities, negativity spoken against me, hatred against me, and any form of self-doubt.

I release the emotional baggage and tension connected to it.

I release and unpack the layers of built-up hurt and resentment.

I AM on the way to my destination.

I AM celebrating my route!

∫ *I felt the weight of carrying multiple bags that were not only mine but also those I put before myself. I prayed for strength, but was it for help carrying those bags or cutting the cords that kept me bound?* ∫

"I AM" My Affirmations

Day Three

I inhale relaxation and exhale tension (repeat 3x's).

I AM free of anxiety, and I AM living a calm life.

I AM no one's placeholder and no longer keep any.

I refuse to cloud the view of who GOD had made for me, nor my own line of sight.

It is well within my power to write my vision and make it plain.

I focus on positivity for a better me.

My talents are limitless.

I see challenges in my life with great clarity.

I AM worthy of respect, and I AM respectful.

Today, I affirm that I AM

_____.

(Fill in the blank.)

∫ *After realizing the invisible pounds I gained, anxiety kept showing up as if it received a never-ending invitation. My getaway was going to the shooting range. Pulling the trigger of the weapon and hearing the shots pacified my anxiety.* ∫

Ebony Wadlington

Day Four

I AM confident that GOD has equipped me with everything I need to accomplish the dream HE has given me.

I have total control over my life.

No weapon formed against me shall prosper.

I AM fearfully and wonderfully made.

∫ *I wanted control over my life*
but did not know how to do it or where to start. ∫

Day Five

Life is not an emergency.

Life will go on.

My plan is not the only plan.

I AM open to allowing myself to be spontaneous.

I AM experiencing peace from letting go.

I AM powerful.

I have incredible strength.

Today, I give myself credit.

This is NOT my endpoint!

∫ I wanted a change to happen at the snap of my fingers, but it did not work. Would anyone care or notice if I were no longer physically present? I was looking for an easy way out to no longer feel. ∫

Ebony Wadlington

Day Six

I AM free—free of negativity!

If it is the wrong energy, it is automatically not for me!

It is BLOCKED!

I AM free of narcissists, manipulators, and liars.

What is for me is already being prepared and en route to me.

I will always win when I move with love's genuine intentions.

I AM free!

∫ *The relationship I was in for three years was "toxic." I was mentally abused more than anything. I lost my self-worth and identity. It was as if I were a stranger in my own house.* ∫

"I AM" My Affirmations

Day Seven

I AM valuable!

I AM secure!

I AM empowered!

I AM a conqueror!

I AM a giant-slayer!

I AM confident!

I AM and will always be enough!

♪ I saw a spectacle of light and was not going to lose it. No looking back. It's time to rebuild. I check my surroundings and find the tools needed to take the steps forward. Words I heard in the church came to mind. I grab hold of them and repeat them until I believe. ♪

Ebony Wadlington

Day Eight

It's OK to feel emotions.

It's OK to self-isolate sometimes.

It's OK to make mistakes.

It's also OK to forgive yourself.

It's OK to love yourself.

It's OK to be Unapologetically Me.

I AM allowed to decide.

∫ *Everyone cannot go where you are headed. I prayed for God to remove anyone who was not good for me. Who would have known I had to let go of people I thought would be in my life until the end? I was depressed at the notion.* ∫

Day Nine

I AM a walking armor...

Unshakable in my convictions...

Insensitive to the negative opinion of everyone who does not have an interest in my goals.

I AM here to grow into the full awareness of my true nature.

Creativity, happiness, and peace are mine!

∫ *The night before, I praise danced in my living room for hours. The next morning, I woke up with a sharp pain and could not walk. I called out for my mother and tried to crawl. The ambulance came and rushed me to the E.R. The doctors found nothing. I fought multiple spiritual battles that night, but my end was not now.* ∫

Ebony Wadlington

Day Ten

I have a life full of reasons to be thankful and happy.

I AM allowed to say "No" to others and "Yes" to myself.

I will take the risk…and have faith.

I AM proud of my strength to walk away from what does not deserve me.

I AM loving on ME, even while I work on ME.

Everything I need will be provided to ME at the right time.

Freedom is ME…

Unapologetically ME.

∫ Where are my people pleasers? "No" was difficult to say and stand on. Friends would call me their "Rider." I was always down, even without knowing the entire story. I often found myself being taken advantage of in situations where I thought I was safe. ∫

"I AM" My Affirmations

Day Eleven

God gave us gifts…

The gift to TEACH.

The gift of JOY.

The gift to HEAL.

The power is in our WORDS.

Sometimes, what blocks us is US.

Do you want to take on the work…the responsibility?

Align yourself to the frequency of what you want to receive.

Believe it is already happening.

Be optimistic and envision your desires.

Practice makes improvement.

May the words of my heart be pleasing to your soul.

∫ I started my hair loc journey, helped plan my mom's retirement, spent quality time with my inner circle, and allowed new connections to enter my life—although there was only one of me. I sometimes had multiple events in one day, and some were not open to sharing their friend. A decision was made, but I found myself explaining my decisions. ∫

Ebony Wadlington

Day Twelve

Today, I give myself permission to...

Get out of my comfort zone.

Ask for help.

Grow and believe in ME.

Remove toxic people from my life.

Release the past.

Step into my greatness.

Shine, be a light, and stand out.

Be loved.

Today, I give myself permission to:

_____.

(Fill in the blank.)

PERMISSION GRANTED!

∫ *You can't talk to everyone about everything. We only have so many hours in a day. Nothing is 100% guaranteed. Failure happens. What's for us will be for US!* ∫

"I AM" My Affirmations

Day Thirteen

Isolation → Transformation

I do not have to be defensive. I know who my Protector is.

I need not one person to validate ME.

GOD has my back!

GOD trusts the power inside of ME.

There is nothing little about ME.

I AM growing.

I have a choice to pick the size. Why not choose BIG?

Have BIG DREAMS and BIG GOALS!

Reach HIGHER.

Expand my mind.

Share, learn, and grow.

I will stay encouraged.

∫ *No one was doubting me but me.*
I must believe it will work out for it to work out. ∫

Ebony Wadlington

Day Fourteen

Today is a GREAT day!

Inhale (1, 2, 3). Exhale (1, 2, 3).

I clear channels of distractions.

I AM radiating positivity.

I AM at peace where I AM today.

I trust myself.

I forgive myself.

My weaknesses turn into my strengths.

I AM fun, fearless, and full of life!

I AM enough, and I AM loved!

∫ *At some point, your courage got to be greater than your fear.* ∫

Day Fifteen

Trust the process.

If it's meant for ME, it will come to ME.

Everything is going to work out with my finances, my health, and my family.

No chasing!

No anxiety!

No stress!

I AM being supported.

I AM trusting the process!

∫ The perception of unemployment can go either way. It was nice not waking up to clock in for someone else. Similarly, I thought about how the bills were going to get paid. I recall getting up early to go to the food pantries and parking down the street so no one would recognize my car. ∫

Ebony Wadlington

Day Sixteen

I AM a vessel full of power.

I have the ingredients needed to reach my goals.

I think positively and envision the future.

I believe it is already happening.

Practice makes improvement.

I get proper rest.

I set the intention and listen to HIS voice.

Aye, happy people do happy people shyt!

∫ *Which one has more power over the other: a college degree or experience? Those with a degree might not get a job because they do not yet have the experience. Those with experience might not get the job because they do not have the credentials.* ∫

"I AM" My Affirmations

Day Seventeen

I will not judge myself about my past. I do not live there anymore.

I can make a simple choice to stand back up and try again...

To love again...

To dream again...

To live again.

No weapon formed against ME shall prosper.

I will break every generational curse.

I AM more than a conqueror.

I walk in my truth without excuse.

I AM fearless and full of life.

My peace is activated.

I write original pages in my book.

I AM enough!

∫ *My longest relationship ended the day he called to tell me his baby was born.* ∫

Ebony Wadlington

Day Eighteen

Happy _____!
(Insert day of the week.)

Choose YOU today! Love YOU today! Let things flow today!

What is meant to be will be.

Lead with love and respect, not ill intentions.

Accept people where they are. Do not try to convince them.

The disrespect is assuming they know what's good for YOU.

Don't tolerate the bully in your relationships. Leave when it no longer serves you—and leave quickly!

Catch the red flags with discernment. Learn the lessons.

GOD gave us the gifts of free will, strength, courage, wisdom, and resilience.

YOU are enough!

YOU are worthy!

YOU MATTER!

∫ *Growing up in a city with no siblings or family members around my age was tough. I was scared and uncomfortable when God showed me things, often questioning, "Why is it happening?" Then, the emotional floodgates would open. I learned the body rejects what is not right.* ∫

"I AM" My Affirmations

Day Nineteen

I give myself permission to grow unapologetically.

If I rush the process, I might ruin the results.

Writing is a powerful enterprise.

I AM unique.

My fingerprints are unique.

My DNA is unique.

I AM an original, not a clone.

My courage is greater than my fear.

There is a difference between existing and living.

Be intentional and live on purpose.

Shyt! Make life happen!

∫ Do you want to see what happens if you don't give up? Look around. Appreciate what you see because it will look different the next time around. Grow daily. Trust your intuition. Do not stress about the past or the future. Love life for what it is and stay present in the moment. ∫

Ebony Wadlington

Day Twenty

Today is a special occasion because I AM alive.

I lead with love.

I run my own race at my own pace.

I AM beautiful in every stage of life.

I AM a magnet for unexpected blessings.

I AM intentional about resting, recharging, and refueling.

My destiny is not average.

I AM authentic in ways that I can explore and express my thoughts.

My presence brings ME excitement!

I love ME!

∫ *You want something better but don't know how to get it. Start from within.* ∫

"I AM" My Affirmations

Day Twenty-One

Today is the BEST day of my life!

I look in the mirror and can see the beauty in my smile.

May my glass go from half-full to full to runneth over!

I ask, listen, and walk in my calling.

Today, I look at life through a fresh lens.

Today, I scope out different mental vantage points.

I will explore the possibilities without worrying about what others might think.

I AM built for it and stronger than it!

I will rise above my circumstances!

♪ Don't be overly attached to the story. Look at it for what it is. ♪

Day Twenty-Two

I AM fully aware of what I control.

My discernment is second-to-none, and I shall not question it.

I AM free of indecision and doubt.

I AM fully capable of clearly seeing what is not for me, and I shall no longer fight it!

I AM at peace.

I AM in a state of complete acceptance of all that is right here, right now!

I AM thankful for what I do have.

My happiness dwells in my soul.

I have an abundance.

I feel great about what I have rather than how much I have.

∫ *A childhood friend of mine who was married and had a child once told me that as adults, we could hang out ONLY if I was married or had a child of my own.* ∫

"I AM" My Affirmations

Day Twenty-Three

I AM beautiful, inside and out.

I smile every chance I get.

My anxiety is calm.

I can see, think, and hear clearly.

Everything that is for ME is en route to ME.

I have no worries.

I have a life partner/soulmate who respects and loves me unconditionally.

Wealthy is my state of mind.

♩ *If you feel undervalued, know that you are not forgotten.* ♩

Ebony Wadlington

Day Twenty-Four

I AM pushing you out!

Anxiety, I AM pushing you out!

Procrastination, I AM pushing you out!

Self-doubt, I AM pushing you out!

Loneliness, I AM pushing you out!

Unforgiveness, I AM pushing you out!

_____, I AM pushing you out!
(Fill in the blank.)

I AM making room for more fire!

∫ *Pain and being misunderstood will happen on your journey.* ∫

"I AM" My Affirmations

Day Twenty-Five

I welcome all the ways my body can be healed.

I give every opinion and option my open mind.

Every time I think healing thoughts, my body responds kindly.

I treat my body—this temple and vessel—with respect.

I AM grateful for the chance to be alive, and I thank my body for giving me this opportunity.

I AM free of diseases. No virus or bacteria can live within me.

I AM on the way to my destination.

I AM celebrating my route!

∫ When my mother was diagnosed with Ulcerative Colitis, we went back and forth to the doctor's office and hospital. Her weight went down to about 85 pounds, and the doctor did not think she was going to make it. ∫

Ebony Wadlington

Day Twenty-Six

My words are powerful.

I forgive myself for past mistakes.

I welcome this new stage in my life.

My own self-care is a priority to ME.

I AM committed to being the best, healthiest ME.

I prefer inner peace more than temporary satisfaction.

I cannot control what happens, but I will make the best choices for ME.

∫ Is something living in your head rent-free? You're only hurting yourself thinking about it, not anyone else. You've given it too much power. Let it go. Go from being in a prison to residing in a palace in your mind and expose yourself to a better environment. ∫

"I AM" My Affirmations

Day Twenty-Seven

I AM debt-free!

My car note is paid in full!

My student loans are paid in full!

My credit cards have a zero balance!

My mortgage is paid off!

My medical bills are no more!

I AM debt-free!

Yes, that's ME...debt-free!

♪ *Do not carry a debt you do not owe.* ♪

Ebony Wadlington

Day Twenty-Eight

When I let go, I create space for better.

My mind acts as a magnet for whatever I want.

I AM focused and organized.

My life is easy and free.

I attract incredible wealth.

My reality is that I procreate.

My manifesting powers are believable.

∫ *Change is not easy for anyone, but it is necessary.* ∫

"I AM" My Affirmations

Day Twenty-Nine

Every day is a new beginning.

I AM focused on what GOD currently has in store for ME.

I allow GOD's positivity, love, strength, and grace to lead.

I AM built for this life.

I forgive myself and others.

I AM powerful alone but a force together.

∫ *Is the battle you are currently facing worth fighting or is it a distraction?* ∫

Ebony Wadlington

Day Thirty

I AM intentional about who I AM, and who I AM not.

I was called to adapt in the time of manifestation.

I AM equipped with the tools and the words.

I step into it with confidence and belief.

I find a way to channel how someone can receive.

I keep growing for change.

I keep pressing.

I have power.

I have been exposed to who I can be in a better environment.

I AM the essence of ME.

∫ *Life doesn't have to rob you of your ability to believe.*
Take back your power! ∫

My "I AM" Affirmations

I hope and pray that those past 30 days have empowered and uplifted you on your life's journey. Use the pages that follow to affirm yourself as often as necessary. Reflect on them periodically, and make a note of your growth along the way!

Ebony Wadlington

"I AM" My Affirmations

Ebony Wadlington

"I AM" My Affirmations

About the Author

Ebony Wadlington was born and raised in Houston, Texas. Growing up as an only child, she was fascinated with music, dance, and writing in her journal, which led to early exposure to dance and culture at the age of five.

Ebony received a bachelor's degree from Texas Southern University and a master's degree from Walden University. She is a humanitarian and servant of God who donated her eggs in 2015 to help a family conceive. Presently, she works in Public Health.

If Ebony isn't spending time with those she loves, you can often find her crocheting, dancing, laughing, supporting others, seeing the bright side in everything, and encouraging those she encounters.

"I AM" My Affirmations is Ebony's first Self-Help book.

Ebony Wadlington

www.ingramcontent.com/pod-product-compliance
Lightning Source LLC
Chambersburg PA
CBHW061515040426
42450CB00008B/1625